For all the little explorers - may your curiosity take you far!

Dedication:

Let's Go LeeAnn is dedicated to my five wonderful children— Derek, Nick, Kyle, Skyler, and Avery—and to my four beautiful grandchildren—Waylon, Virginia, Lillianna, and Diana—with three more on the way at the time of publication!

Reading stories to my children, and now my grandchildren, has always been one of my greatest joys. I've cherished every giggle, question, and moment of wonder we've shared through books.

Writing has long been a passion of mine, and what better way to bring that passion to life than by creating stories that spark imagination and connection for young readers everywhere.

LET'S GO LEEANN - ZOO

Hi friends!

I'm back for another adventure!
Are you ready?

Let's go!

Today, we're going to the zoo to visit some of our favorite animal friends.

My favorite animal is the giraffe.

What's your favorite animal?

Giraffes have long necks to reach the tops of trees and eat yummy leaves.

They also have super-long tongues-almost as long as your arm!

Stick out your tongue-how long is yours?

Look at the elephants! They're so big!

They use their trunks like straws-to drink water, grab food and even give hugs!

Over here we see the penguins waddling around wearing tiny tuxedos.

Did you know penguin daddies help take care of the eggs?

They keep the eggs warm until the chick hatches.

What's another animal
that lays eggs?

Who likes monkeys?

"No more monkeys jumping on the bed!"

Monkeys swing from tree to tree and love munching on bananas.

Do you like bananas too?

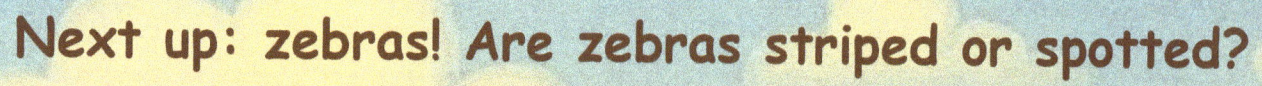

Next up: zebras! Are zebras striped or spotted?

That's right-striped! They eat grass, shrubs, and leaves and can run super fast!

Do you know the fastest animal on land?

It's the cheetah!

Cheetahs are the fastest land animals and can run faster than a car!

They are covered in spots and love to chase after their food.

Let's go find some bears.

There are many kinds-brown bears, polar bears, grizzly bears, and panda bears!

Bears love to eat...and nap.

Some sleep for over
100 days without
food or water.

Could you sleep
that long?

shhh!

Can you say hippopotamus? That's a big word!

We call them hippos for short.

Hippos love the water and their babies,
called calves, like to ride on their backs.

Do you like swimming too?

Now look-there's a pink bird! It's a flamingo!

Flamingos stand on one leg and get their pink color from eating shrimp and algae.

Can you balance on one leg like a flamingo?

Wow, that was so much fun!

We saw so many animals and learned amazing things.

But it's time to let our zoo friends rest.

Say bye-bye, animals! See you again soon!

Let's Go LeeAnn

Tonya Elizabeth

Match the Animal to Its Home

(Draw lines or use stickers to connect animals to their habitats)

Ice/Snow

Savannah

Forest

Wetlands

Which Animals Lay Eggs?

Circle the animals that lay eggs.

Help LeeAnn find her way to the giraffe!

START

ZOO

FINISH

Draw Your Favorite Zoo Animal!

Who wants to go to the farm?
Join the adventure in Let's Go LeeAnn - Farm

Packed with fun, learning, and farmyard friends —
it's a journey your little ones won't want to miss!